Fifty Grades of Pay

B G Knoll

Fifty Grades of Pay: How to ask for *and get* the raise you deserve

Copyright © 2021 B G Knoll and 800 Muses Publishing

All rights reserved. In accordance with the U.S. Copyright Act of 1976, the scanning, uploading, and electronic sharing of any part of this book without the permission of the author or publisher constitutes unlawful piracy and theft of the author's intellectual property. If you would like to use material from the book (other than for review purposes), prior written permission must be obtained by contacting the publisher.

800 Muses Publishing
800Muses.com

Printed in the United States of America

If you don't ask, the answer is always no.

— Nora Roberts

Fifty Grades of Pay

You're having a dream and all you can see are clouds and mist. As the mist clears, you realize you're inside an unfamiliar mansion, standing at the entrance of a grand hall. To your left, you notice a corridor, and something compels you to walk toward it. As you approach, you see that the corridor is long and has no exits until the very end where there is an ornately carved wooden door. The floor is white marble, and the corridor is cold; your body starts to tense as walk toward the door. Your tension mounts as you approach and you can feel your heart in your throat, but finally you stand outside the door upon which you see affixed a small brass plaque that reads:

        IF YOU OPEN THIS DOOR,

        EITHER NOTHING WILL HAPPEN,

        OR SOMETHING VERY GOOD WILL HAPPEN.

Any chance you're *not* going to open that door?

If you ask for a raise, either nothing will happen, or *you'll get the raise.*

If you've been wanting a raise and have been afraid to ask for one, you're not alone. Most people would rather walk over hot coals than go to their boss with their hand out, possibly risking their job in the process. But here's the truth: According to Marketplace.com, 74% of women who ask for a raise get one, and 82% of men do.

But Marketplace also found that only 37% of men and 36% of women ask. Why? According to FastCompany.com, there are four primary reasons, and they all boil down to fear:

1. Fear that you don't deserve the money
2. Fear of rejection
3. Fear of negotiating
4. Fear of losing your job

It's Okay to Ask—In Fact, It's Your Duty to Ask

Can you imagine any vendor you've ever worked with not increasing its prices over time? Your value to your company increases with every day you put in. You're worth much more after six months than you were at Day 1, and much more after six years than at the end of Year 1. It's neither greedy nor entitled to ask for a raise. In fact, if you don't ask for a raise, your manager may eventually wonder about your value. Asking for a raise demonstrates your confidence in your self-worth. Increasing your salary demonstrates your employer's investment in you, and we all value our investments. The mere factor of confidently asking for a raise is likely to raise your value in your manager's eyes.

You may think it's your manager's responsibility to recognize your contributions and reward you accordingly. It's not your manager's responsibility—it's yours.

Managers are torn between keep their employees happy and keeping their own managers happy. If you're excelling at your position, it makes them look good, and they're great with that, but they may not connect that with the need to reward you.

Preparation is Required

To paraphrase Edison, who said *genius is 1% inspiration and 99% perspiration,* asking for a raise is 1% asking and 99% *tasking.* Tasking means work—work that will give the *asking* a much better chance of success.

Task 1: Research

Research salaries for the positions in your field. Not just your position, but your position in the industry and location in which you work. The pay scale for a project manager may be $60K in one industry, $120K in another, and $240K in a high-cost location. Talk to recruiters in your area. Describe your position and ask in what salary range they're placing candidates. In doing so, know this: Many recruiters will not give out salary ranges to actual candidates. As one recruiter explained, *"For one thing, we want to pay up to mid-point and not much above. Anything above [midpoint] requires additional approvals."*

Not only do salaries vary widely by industry and location, they rarely tell the full picture. Before relying on a salary range you find on Glassdoor, or a job posting on Indeed, research the company and look at its compensation package. An NGO that pays lower salaries may offer a 15% match to its 403b; companies may offer annual bonuses of as much as 50% of base pay; and there may be other compensating factors, such as stock options.

Did you know Colorado law requires employers to post the salary ranges for their open positions or incur a sizable fee? But know this: Whenever most companies post salaries, they will post in the low- to mid-range. If they can get qualified candidates at that price, they will. This doesn't mean this range is the top price a company is willing to pay, however.

Network. Take a colleague from a competitor company to lunch. While you don't want to discuss salaries among your own company (this is often a fireable offense) doing so should not be taboo among competitors. You'll learn more from a colleague in a similar position at another company than you will from online job postings. "The Cut.com" recommends, rather than asking, *"How much do you earn?"* you instead ask, *"What would you expect a job like X at a company like Y to pay?"* You could also ask, *"What have you learned about the pay scale for our position, and what do you think is reasonable?"*

When researching your position and salary, don't overlook the job descriptions. Does it match your current responsibilities? You may well find that you're being compensated at a manager level when you're doing the work of a vice president.

Task 2: Gather Your Data

This is a tip for the rest of your career: Keep a file folder with kudos and accomplishments and add to it consistently, especially any contributions you make related to your manager's pet projects.

Example

> Mara knew that customer surveys were a key focus for her manager. However, they received little notice from the rest of the team because reviewing them wasn't an integral part of their roles. Mara made a point of checking the surveys each month and following up on any pain points of her customers. She also kept a record of the increase in overall customer satisfaction ratings and was able to tie the increase to the work she did.

In addition to the salary range you've found (and other benefits), compile a list of your own selling points:

- How long has it been since you've had a salary increase?
- What quantifiable metrics demonstrate your worth to the organization?
- How long have you been a loyal employee?
- Where have you gone above and beyond on the job, and how has that positively impacted the company's bottom line?
- What intangible but valuable contributions have you made?
    - Positive feedback from other departments, particularly other department managers on the same level (or above) as your manager
    - Additional responsibilities you've taken on
    - Additional direct reports you now manage
- What are your plans for contributing to your company in the near future? Help your manager see not just how valuable you've been but how valuable you're about to be. For instance, if your company is taking on a new vertical, your job responsibilities will be expanding.
- How is what you do on the job making your manager's job easier or more effective?

Task 3: Know Your Number

Have in mind a specific number you want (percentage or dollar amount) and be prepared to support it. Without that number, you're essentially saying, *"I deserve a raise. How about it?"* If there were an ejector seat for your raise, that would trigger it. Have a definite number. Always tie the request to your performance. And keep in mind that your manager's job is to save the company money, which includes not losing you, but may not include giving you everything you ask for. Plan to ask for 15% more than you expect to get, because that's likely how much your number—if considered—will be discounted.

According to Business News Daily, the average pay raise is 3%, with 4.5% to 6% being "good" and anything above that considered "exceptional." However, if the data you've collected justifies it, asking for a 10-20% raise is perfectly reasonable.

Task 4: Rehearse

This is one of the most important presentations you'll make all year, so prepare for it. Decide what you're going to say and have your talking points all worked out in advance.

Don't make it personal; this is a professional meeting. Don't say, "My wife just had a baby ..." or "my son just entered college." And don't take 100% credit for teamwork. You can say, "I contributed to the success of the Production Department by reducing overhead costs by 17%. This saved the company $163,172." (Precise numbers are better because they show you've done your homework.)

Rehearse your presentation. Ask a partner, spouse, or friend to listen, taking on the role of your manager. Prepare the person in advance by providing them with what public relations agencies call a "rude Q&A." This is a list of the most difficult questions members of the press might ask the agencies' clients. In your case, make a list of the objections your manager is likely to make. Then decide how you will respond professionally and firmly to each of these questions.

Examples and possible responses follow.

- **Q: I'd really like to give you a raise, but you're already at the top of your salary range.**
  A: Here's the data I've found on salary ranges for my position in our industry. If it requires a promotion to be compensated at this level, I'm ready. I'm already contributing at a higher level than my current position as the following examples will show...

- **Q: If I give you a raise, everyone will want one.**
  A: I'm asking to be paid according to my value to the company. Over the last year, my contributions include …
- **Q: The company is trying to operate lean right now.**
  A: We just landed a big contract with X. I expect to contribute on an even higher level going forward so we can capitalize on that opportunity. Here are the plans I have for doing just that …

Avoid modifiers. *I'm asking for* is fine because it's firm and states your position. *I believe, I want,* and *I feel* aren't. These sound apologetic, and you have nothing to apologize for. This is business.

Here's a sample outline for your presentation. Tailor it to your own situation.
1. Start with the background of your time with the company and a mention of how much you value contributing to the organization's success.
2. Share highlights of your recent contributions.
3. Provide current salary data for your position, and (if it builds your case) mention how long it's been since your last increase.
4. State that you'd like your salary to match your level of contribution and *state your number.*
5. Close with your plans on how you intend to contribute in the future.

You don't need to a verbatim script, but you should put a few key phrases in your back pocket to pull out. Politicians do this all the time, creating memorable sound bites.

Should You Make Your Request in Writing?

Whenever possible, it's best to have an in-person meeting with your manager, even if it must be by Zoom. But there may be times when you need to make your request in writing, and there may be advantages for doing so, such as creating a formal request. And you may need to make a written request to schedule the salary discussion, in which case you're going to have to let your manager know what the discussion is about.

How should you word this written communication? If your request for a raise must be in writing, you won't be able to cover everything you could in an in-person meeting, so stick to the basics. Beware of templated letters you find online, however. Sample letters posted on TemplateLAB, for instance, are exceptionally instructive for what *not* to write.

Verbatim excerpts from these templates are included below.

Don't write:

> *I strongly feel that I have earned this pay raise. If you do not feel that way, I understand.*

Instead, be firm, professional, and positive.

> *I'm writing to formally request a review of my salary.*
>
> *I believe a review of my recent accomplishments [briefly list] justifies an increase of X%.*
>
> *Recent additional duties I've assumed are [list].*
>
> *In [recent month/year] I managed the successful launch of [X], resulting in a $X increase in sales.*

Don't write:

> *My salary is below the industry averages for the competencies I possess.*
>
> *Though I am grateful for the professional opportunities the company offers me, I regret to tell you that my current salary doesn't meet my expectations.*

Instead of generalities and complaints, be specific, and provide real data.

> *According to [authoritative source], the industry average for my position and level of experience is [$X].*

If your written communication is by email, TheBalanceCareers.com suggests the following strategy.

Don't discuss a specific dollar amount. Instead, your email message should include:

- A request for a meeting to discuss your compensation (put this in the subject line of the message)
- Why you deserve a salary increase
- What additional responsibilities you have taken on in your role
- Any skills or certifications you have acquired since being hired

Mindset is Crucial

If you know you deserve a raise (if you've done your research and prepared your data and know what you're going to say), it will give you confidence. Put yourself in your manager's position: You're helping your company retain a valuable and loyal employee, and you're likely saving it money in the long run. A 2017 report by Employee Benefits News found that turnover can cost employers 33% of an employee's annual salary. Lost productivity and increased compensation are likely.

Loyalty is another factor. According to the U.S. Bureau of Statistics, the average turnover rate in the U.S. is 12-15% annually. If you've proved your loyalty, you are a known entity, and a replacement may cost the company untold expenses in compensation and turnover.

As one learning professional shared, "I asked my company for a raise that I richly deserved. Management said no, so I left. Every candidate they interviewed afterward wanted more than I'd asked for."

However, don't threaten to quit. This can backfire and it makes you look unprofessional. It's fine, however, to say something like, "I love the work

I do here and would like to remain with the company long-term. That said, my understanding of the market is that I should be making $X" or "I'm contributing at a higher level than my current job title. Here are some examples …"

Keep your goals in mind. Consider the good you can do for your family with a salary increase, or the good you can do for the causes you believe in. Keep that thought in mind if asking for an increase on your own behalf isn't enough motivation for you.

Ask for a Meeting and Time It Well

Strategic timing of your request for a salary increase can either improve or impede your chance for success. Indeed.com offers this advice. *"If you know that your manager is under a lot of stress or focused on too many things right now, it may not be the time to ask for a raise. Paying attention to your manager's moods and identifying how to help them demonstrates a level of maturity that will be useful to mention in your conversation about compensation."*

A good time to ask for a raise is at the end of the fiscal year prior to budgeting and reporting purposes. The management team will be determining compensation and hiring costs at that time.

You may decide to time your ask for your next performance review, but if that's not for several months and the timing is otherwise beneficial (your company just landed a big contract), strike while the iron is hot. The beginning of a new project is not the time the company wants to lose a valuable employee.

When you ask your manager for a sit-down, it's best to disclose the topic of conversation. No one likes to be caught off-guard. On the other hand, if you're prepared and the opportunity presents itself for an uninterrupted closed-door meeting, you may want to state your case. When you ask to meet, it's likely your manager will be thinking, *"This employee is either going to quit, bring me a personnel problem, or ask for a raise."* The raise is the least of your manager's worries.

After the Ask

If, after you've made your presentation, your manager is unable to give you an answer right away (it may require additional approvals, for instance), be gracious. Thank your manager for the time and consideration and give it a few days. However, if you haven't heard back within a week, it's fine to check in.

The Cut.com offers this tip:

If you know your manager will need to get your increase approved at another level, such as a higher-level manager or HR, you can make it easier for your manager to obtain that approval by providing a short, bulleted list of key points in your favor. It's recommended to keep this to one page of highlights of your most significant new responsibilities or contributions, assigning a dollar value (increase in company's bottom line) whenever possible. On this brief document, include the competitive salary data you've found.

While waiting for an answer, dress professionally, come to work on time, collaborate well with colleagues, be prepared for every team meeting, contribute well considered ideas, and be a top producer in your position.

What if the Answer is No?

As part of the "rude Q&A" you prepare with your role-playing partner, decide what you're going to say whether your manager answers "yes," "no," or "maybe." Have a well-considered response for each scenario.

If you get a no, consider whether you've stated your case thoroughly enough. You may have to try a different tack in a month or two, armed with more data. In the meantime, you can do the following:

- Ask your manager what it would take to earn a raise in the future, and whether you can set a date to discuss it then. If there's no response, you've hit a dead end on salary for that position. You may want to begin grooming yourself for a new position in that company or elsewhere.
- See if you can negotiate other aspects of your compensation (e.g., company stock, extra vacation days, work from home opportunities).

Don't ask for a counteroffer. Your manager now knows you're dissatisfied with your current salary and may be looking for a new position. If your manager doesn't offer a salary bump of some kind, introducing a lower number at this point isn't going to help.

If you're stonewalled and are given little hope that things will change, you may want to look for another job. Those connections you made with competitors and recruiters during your research phase may now pay off.

As one recruiting veteran put it: *"Sadly, the best way to get a raise is often to take a new job with a new company."*

BONUS CONTENT

Tips from the U.S. Bureau of Labor and Statistics When Applying for a New Position

Preparation

Career counselors say a good job interview starts well before the jobseeker and interviewer meet. Preparation can be as important as the interview itself. Researching, practicing, and dressing appropriately are the first steps to making the most of a job interview.

Research. Learning about the company and the position for which you are being interviewed is essential—and it will help you to show employers that you are really interested.

Before arriving for an interview, you should know what the company does and any recent changes it has undergone. Learn about the company's mission and goals. With these in mind, you can show during the interview how your qualifications match the company's needs.

The company itself is often the easiest place to start your research. Many businesses have information on their websites that's tailored to jobseekers. But don't stop there: In-depth research is important. Read news publications, trade journals, and other sources of information to learn more about the company.

Employment and social media sites, especially those related to business networking, may have more specific information about the company's culture. For example, current and former employees may post reviews of the employer or offer details about questions they were asked during a job interview.

Practice. Another important step in preparing for a job interview is to practice describing your professional characteristics. Think of examples from past jobs, schoolwork, and activities to illustrate important skills. Recalling accomplishments beforehand, when you are not being evaluated, helps you to give solid answers during the interview.

Every interview is different, and it's always possible there will be questions that surprise you. Nevertheless, interviewers suggest rehearsing with a career counselor or a friend to build confidence and poise. As a starting point, try answering these questions aloud:

What are your strengths and weaknesses?

Can you tell me about a time you dealt with conflict as part of a team?

Why did you leave, or are you leaving, your job?

What are your goals?

Why should we hire you?

Each question allows you to illustrate your favorable characteristics. When responding, focus on subjects related to the job. For example, if asked to describe yourself, talk about your professional characteristics and background, not your personal life.

Some questions, such as those about hobbies or interests, may seem irrelevant. Interviewers ask these types of questions to learn about your personality and test your interpersonal skills. These questions also let you highlight some of your other strengths. Participating in a sport might demonstrate teamwork, for example. And ability in a craft, such as jewelry making, might show your attention to detail.

Whatever the question, emphasize the positive. If there is a weakness evident on your résumé or transcript, such as being fired from a job or receiving poor grades, rehearse an explanation before the interview in case you are asked about them. Focus on what you learned from the experience, and be careful never to criticize a previous employer or coworker.

Look professional. Dress for an interview as you would for an important day on the job, such as a meeting with a supervisor or a presentation to a client. Don't let your appearance distract the interviewer from your qualifications.

Keep your hair neat, and cover any tattoos or piercings, if possible. Avoid cologne and perfume, large pieces of jewelry, and heavy or unnatural makeup. Clothes should be clean, ironed, and fit well. And shoes should be polished and closed-toe.

Many employers expect jobseekers to wear a suit—preferably one in a conservative color such as navy blue, gray, or black—but not all do. A company with an informal dress code might be fine with your wearing a button-down shirt and dress slacks. If you're not sure about what to wear, dressing up is more prudent than dressing down.

Showtime

On the day of the interview, give yourself plenty of time to get ready for and travel to the interview. Plan to arrive 10 to 15 minutes early. (Some career counselors suggest making a test run to the interview site in advance to familiarize yourself with the travel route.)

Consider carrying a folder or briefcase to the interview so you have access to things you'll want while you're there. These include a pen and paper to record important information, such as the proper spelling of the interviewer's name and the time and date of follow-up interviews; copies of your résumé or application and references; and examples of your work, such as writing samples.

Similarly, have these items within easy reach for interviews conducted over the phone or through videoconference. For phone interviews, consider disabling call waiting on the day of the interview; you don't want to put the interviewer on hold, and persistent call-waiting beeps may distract you. For videoconference interviews, make sure that the Web camera is angled correctly and that the surrounding area is neat.

Nervousness. It's natural to feel nervous when interviewing. But remember: You have skills the employer needs. The interview is your chance to show how those skills would be a good fit for the job.

To reduce nervousness, interviewers recommend getting a good night's sleep and maintaining your usual morning routine. If you never eat breakfast, for example, don't eat a hearty morning meal on interview day. They also recommend putting yourself in a positive mindset before the interview by calling to mind some of your happiest memories or proudest moments.

And they remind jobseekers that each opening you interview for is not the only one that exists. There are openings with other companies that might be a better fit. Every interview is an opportunity to practice getting more comfortable talking about yourself.

First impressions. An in-person interview begins the moment you arrive. Everyone you meet, from the receptionist to the hiring manager, will form an impression of you. To ensure the impression is positive, remember that your words and mannerisms affect how others perceive you.

- When greeting people, smile and shake hands.
- Make eye contact and maintain good posture.
- Don't use slang or give curt, one-word answers.
- Don't chew gum, bite your nails, or use your phone.

Making a positive impression is just as important when you interview remotely. Remember to speak clearly and listen attentively, just as you would if you were meeting with the interviewer in person. Even if no one can see you, your voice betrays attitudes and confidence; sometimes, sitting up straight helps to project enthusiasm.

Standard politeness is important in an interview because the interviewer knows little about you. For example, don't presume that you should use your interviewer's first name just because the company atmosphere is relaxed.

Responding to questions. After introductions, the interviewer may explain the job in more detail, discuss the company, or initiate friendly conversation. The interviewer will then ask questions to gauge how well you would fill the position.

When responding to the interviewer, avoid vague answers, such as, *"I want to work with people"* (or animals, or cars, or whatever the job entails). Instead, describe the specific ways you want to work with them, perhaps by giving examples of how you have successfully done so in the past. Focus on your strengths, but be honest.

Let the interviewer direct the session. He or she may use your resume as a guide and ask for additional details. Listen attentively, and answer each question completely. Pay attention to the interviewer's mannerisms for clues about whether to elaborate or to keep your responses short.

Some jobseekers are so focused on specific answers that they forget to relax and connect with the interviewer. An interview should be conversational. However, that doesn't mean you're expected to speak without pause. Stop to consider an answer before responding to difficult or unexpected questions. And if a question is confusing, ask for clarification.

In a group or panel interview, try to engage the whole group. When interviewing with other candidates for a job, take initiative in responding to questions—but be careful not to dominate the discussion.

Turning the tables. At some point, usually toward the end of the interview, you will have the opportunity to ask your own questions. Use this time to learn more about the position—and, often, the person who would be your boss. After all, you're also deciding whether you want the job.

Questions you might want to ask include:

What do you expect me to accomplish in my first 6 months?

Can you describe a typical assignment for this position?

What kind of employee training do you provide?

Will this position lead to advancement opportunities?

What do you like most about working for this company?

An interview is not the time to inquire about salary or benefits; the best time to discuss those topics is after you have been offered the job. You don't want to seem more interested in financial rewards than in contributing to the company. If asked about salary requirements, try to convey flexibility.

Before leaving the interview, make sure you understand the next step in the hiring process. Find out whether there will be another round of interviews, whether you should provide additional information, and when a hiring decision will be made.

And remember to thank the interviewer at the end of the interview.

Following up

Even after the interview is over, an important task remains: Secure a good impression by sending a thank you letter to the interviewer, preferably within 2 days.

Thank you letters should be brief—a few paragraphs if emailed, less than one page if typed or handwritten. Thank the interviewer for the opportunity, briefly reiterate your skills, and confirm your enthusiasm for the job.

Address the letter to the person who interviewed you, and make sure to spell his or her name correctly. If a group interviewed you, write either to each person you spoke with or to the person who led and coordinated the interview, mentioning the other people you met. Be sure to proofread the letter, and ask someone else to proofread it, too.

If you don't hear back within the time frame the interviewer specified, call or email to check on your status. Making that extra effort could mean the difference in getting the job—or not.

A few key takeaways that help teach you how to get the job you want:

Practice describing your work and educational history, accomplishments, and weaknesses. You want to appear confident in both your answers and your delivery.

Questions about hobbies might seem innocuous, but they're actually used to assess your interpersonal skills and help the interviewer glean more insight into who you are as a person and not just as an employee.

That old adage "dress for the job you want" still holds water. Show up groomed and attired in a way that keeps the focus on your words rather than your outfit.

Close Strong

End your interview as powerfully as you began it. When you feel that things are winding down, feel free to ask the interviewer whether they feel you're a good fit and what the next steps may look like. Bonus points for asking if you can connect via LinkedIn and if it's acceptable to check in as things develop. Leave them with a firm handshake and let them know you appreciate their time.

Perfect the Art of the Follow-up

It's safe to assume that you're not the only person being interviewed for a job opening, so how do you stay top-of-mind once you're out of the room? Sending a follow-up indicates you're serious about the position, and it also gives you a chance to remind recruiters of who you are and why you're the best choice. Go for a handwritten thank-you note if possible, but email works as well, and feel free to check in periodically if the hiring process is moving at a snail's pace.

References and Resources

References

Barstow, D. (2018, June 29). *If You Don't Ask, the Answer is Always No.* Psychology Today. https://www.psychologytoday.com/us/blog/ink-blots-cartoons/201806/if-you-dont-ask-the-answer-is-always-no

Cole, S. (2014, October 16). *How To Get Over The 4 Common Fears That Hold People Back From Asking For A Raise.* Fast Company. https://www.fastcompany.com/3037138/how-to-get-over-the-4-common-fears-that-hold-people-back-f

Doyle, A. (2020, September 20). *What Is the Best Way to Ask for a Raise via Email?* The Balance Careers. https://www.thebalancecareers.com/sample-email-message-asking-for-a-raise-2062776

Green, A. (2019, March 12). *How to Ask for a Raise.* The Cut. https://www.thecut.com/article/how-to-ask-for-a-raise.html

Hall, J. (2019, May 9). *The Cost Of Turnover Can Kill Your Business And Make Things Less Fun.* Forbes. https://www.forbes.com/sites/johnhall/2019/05/09/the-cost-of-turnover-can-kill-your-business-and-make-things-less-fun/?sh=3d313dee7943

How to Ask for a Raise (With Script Examples). (2020, November 23). Indeed Career Guide. https://www.indeed.com/career-advice/pay-salary/guide-how-to-ask-for-a-raise

Jackson, A. E. (2020, December 11). *9 Things to Never Say in a Salary Negotiation.* Glassdoor Blog. https://www.glassdoor.com/blog/9-things-to-never-say-in-a-salary-negotiation/

L. (2019, May 5). *50 Best Salary Increase Letters (How To Ask For A Raise?).* TemplateLab. https://templatelab.com/salary-increase-letters/

Martin, M. (2019, November 22). *How to Ask Your Boss for a Raise: 5 Tips for Success*. Business News Daily. https://www.businessnewsdaily.com/8101-asking-for-a-raise-tips.html

Zojceska, A. (2020, April 3). *HR Metrics: How and Why to Calculate Employee Turnover Rate?* Blog. https://www.talentlyft.com/en/blog/article/242/hr-metrics-how-and-why-to-calculate-employee-turnover-rate#:%7E:text=According%20to%20the%20U.S.%20Bureau,above%20the%20average%20turnover%20rates

Resources

- https://www.glassdoor.com
- https://www.payscale.com
- https://www.salary.com

From the Author

Please let me know your results as you leave a review for this book on Amazon. If you can't leave a five-star review, please leave whatever review you feel is appropriate, and let me what I could have done differently to earn five stars from you. I'm committed to success in every aspect of my life and will use your comments to improve this guide.

I wish you five-star success in your career and every aspect of your life!

~ B G

www.ingramcontent.com/pod-product-compliance
Lightning Source LLC
Chambersburg PA
CBHW031522210526
45464CB00007B/3008